Teeth

Greg Pyers

Contents

Rigby

A Harcourt Achieve Imprint

www.Rigby.com
1-800-531-5015

D1262020

Different Teeth

Many animals have teeth. Teeth come in many types.

There are big teeth and small teeth , sharp teeth ,

and flat teeth . There are long teeth and short

teeth, white teeth , and yellow teeth .

2

Now let's look at human teeth. How many different kinds of teeth do we have?

Your front teeth are for biting. They are called **incisors**. There are four pointed teeth next to the incisors. These are **canine** teeth.

Behind your canine teeth are teeth for chewing. These are called **molars**.

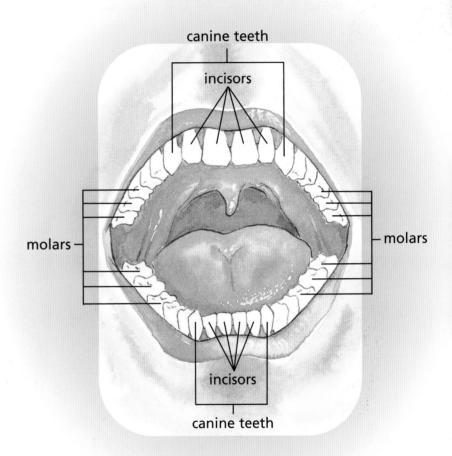

canine teeth

incisors

molars

molars

incisors

canine teeth

Teeth Are Tools

Animals use their teeth in different ways.
Some animals use their teeth to send messages.
Some animals use their teeth to cut through things.

This pygmy chimpanzee is showing it is frightened.

This beaver is cutting through a tree with its teeth.

Some animals use their teeth to carry things.
Some animals use their teeth to fight.

This tiger is taking her cub
to a safe place.

These seals are fighting
for territory on the beach.

Most importantly, animals use their teeth to catch and eat their food.

Teeth for Grinding

Have you ever tried to chew grass? Chewing grass is very difficult because grass is tough and stringy. Cows eat lots of grass every day. How do they do it?

Let's take a closer look.

A cow grabs a clump of grass with its tongue. It pulls the clump and cuts it free with its incisors. A cow then chews the grass with its molars. These teeth are flat and wide.

When the cow chews, its **jaw** moves from side to side, grinding the grass. Soon, the grass is soft and ready to swallow.

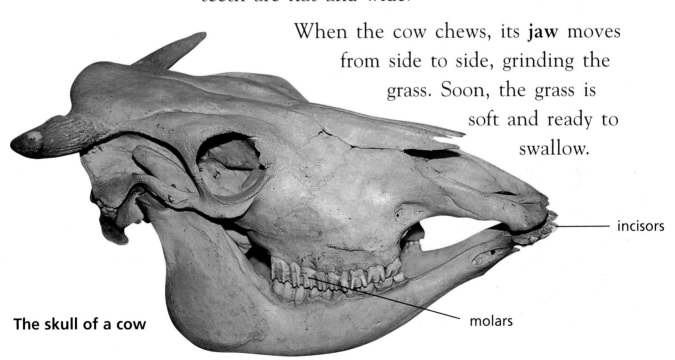

The skull of a cow

incisors

molars

Teeth for Cutting

Lions use their teeth to kill and eat other animals. How does a lion eat its **prey**?

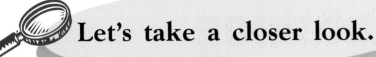
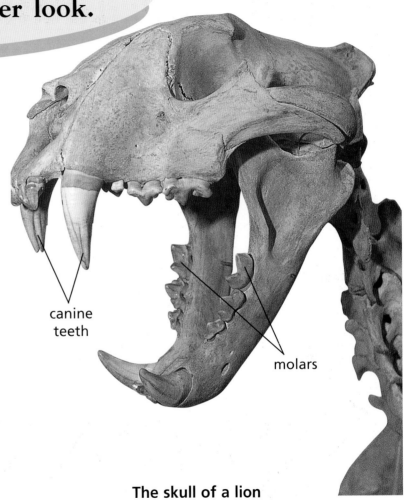

The lion uses its huge canine teeth to grip and kill its prey. The lion's molars are also very sharp. They work like huge scissors. The lion uses its molars to cut through skin, meat, and bone.

canine teeth

molars

The skull of a lion

9

Teeth for Catching

Have you ever held a fish in your hands? They are very slippery. Dolphins eat fish—lots of them! How does a dolphin hold on to its fish?

Let's take a closer look.

A dolphin has rows of pointed teeth. These teeth are like sharp pegs that stick into a slippery fish. A dolphin doesn't have chewing teeth. The dolphin just swallows the fish whole and chases after another one.

The skull of a dolphin

A dolphin has sharp, pointy teeth.

Teeth for Gnawing

A walnut has a hard, wooden shell, but the nut inside is soft and tasty. Squirrels like to eat walnuts. But how does a squirrel break through the shell?

Let's take a closer look.

The squirrel holds a walnut with its front paws. It uses its very long and sharp incisors to **gnaw** through the wooden shell. The squirrel can then reach the food inside.

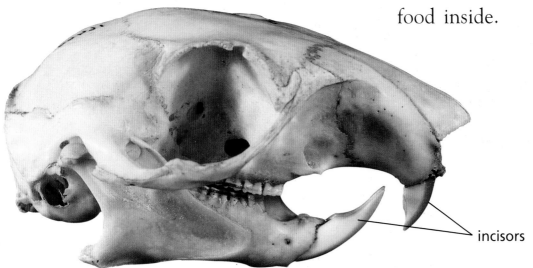

incisors

The skull of a squirrel (enlarged to show detail)

Teeth for Holding

A python is a snake that eats mice, rats, and other small animals. But with no arms or legs, how does a python hold on to its prey?

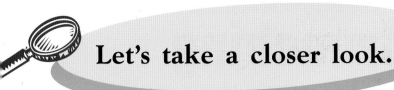

A python has rows of sharp, curved teeth. These teeth are like hooks that stick into food.

Many snakes are **venomous** although the python is not. Venomous snakes use special teeth called fangs to inject venom. Their fangs are hollow so, when the snake bites the prey, the venom enters the prey's body.

The skull of a python

15

Teeth for Crunching

This bat is hunting for its prey—moths. You might think that the bat would find a moth soft and easy to eat. A moth doesn't have any bones. But it has a tough, outer skin called a **cuticle**. How does a bat eat a moth?

The bat uses its sharp, pointed teeth to crunch the moth's cuticle. Its molars then chew the moth's body. The bat is a very small animal, and its jaws are not very strong. Its teeth do all the hard work.

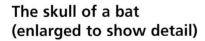

**The skull of a bat
(enlarged to show detail)**

A close-up of the sharp pointed teeth of a bat.

Teeth for Sifting

This seal eats **krill**. Krill are very small shrimp, no bigger than insects. Millions of krill live together in huge swarms in the sea. How does this seal catch such small prey?

The seal opens its mouth and seawater and krill flow in. Then the seal closes its teeth and pushes its tongue against its teeth. The seawater is pushed out, but the krill are trapped inside. To catch krill, the seal uses its teeth like a **sieve**.

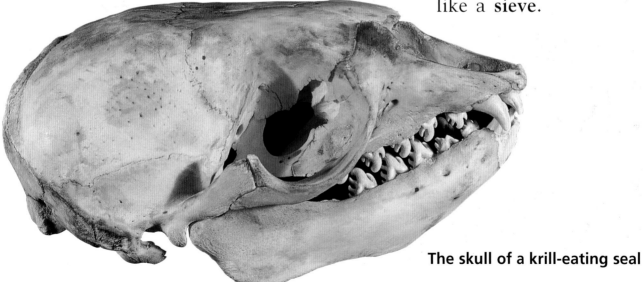

The skull of a krill-eating seal

Fossil Teeth

Millions of years after an animal has died, all that may be left are its teeth. This is because they are covered with **enamel**. Enamel is harder than the hardest bones.

These teeth are **fossil** teeth. Everything else, even the bones, may have rotted away.

Prehistoric animals lived on Earth millions of years ago. Scientists know what they ate by looking at the shape of the animal's teeth.

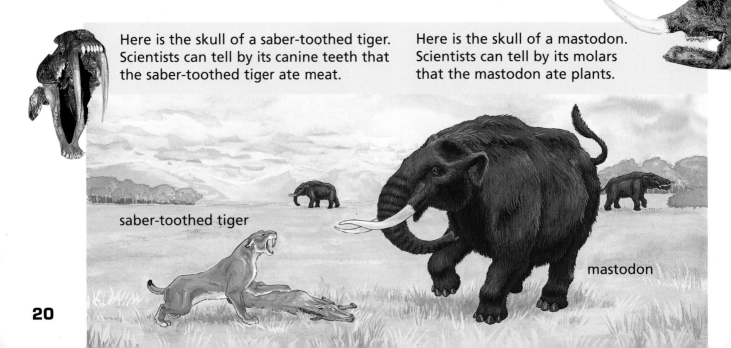

Here is the skull of a saber-toothed tiger. Scientists can tell by its canine teeth that the saber-toothed tiger ate meat.

Here is the skull of a mastodon. Scientists can tell by its molars that the mastodon ate plants.

saber-toothed tiger

mastodon

You Be the Scientist

This 100-million-year-old skull is part of a dinosaur's skeleton that was discovered in South Africa in 1998. Look closely at its teeth.

What sort of food do you think this animal ate? Look at its teeth. Compare them to the teeth of the animals below.

Did the dinosaur have grinding teeth, like a cow's teeth?

Did the dinosaur have cutting teeth, like a lion's teeth?

Did the dinosaur have catching teeth, like a dolphin's teeth?

This dinosaur had a long snout and sharp, pointed teeth. These teeth were well-suited to catching fish. So the dinosaur had teeth most like those of a dolphin. This dinosaur weighed five tons and was more than 11 yards long. It must have eaten quite a lot of fish!

Glossary

canine   canine means "like a dog"

cuticle   the tough skin of an insect

enamel   hard material on the outside of a tooth

fangs   hollow teeth that can inject venom

fossil   the remains of an animal that died long ago

gnaw   using teeth to cut away hard material, such as wood

incisor   a cutting tooth at the front of an animal's mouth

jaw   a bone that holds an animal's teeth

krill   small, shrimp-like sea animals

molar   a tooth at the back of an animal's mouth

prehistoric   to do with the time in history before information was written down

prey   animals that are eaten by other animals

sieve   a round container with small holes used for separating food from liquid such as water

venomous   poisonous

Index